How To Negotiate With The IRS and Win!

Your GPS Roadmap to Settling IRS Delinquencies on <u>Your</u> Terms Fast.

James A. Gage. MTx

"A delinquent Tax obligation is like a scarlet letter. Once you have one you carry it around damaging your financial well being. But, now there is hope! Certain tax laws and procedures allow you to negotiate your tax obligations on your terms. This book has the answers. Read it. Start getting your financial life back."

Prof. Alan M. Dershowitz

Harvard Law Professor and the man Time Magazine calls "the top lawyer of last resort in the country".

James A. Gage, JAG Publications

Copyright © 2013

All rights reserved.

ISBN-10: 0615770479
ISBN-13: 978-0615770475 (JAG Publications)

Disclaimer

We, GCG, LLC, James Gage, Negotiating For A Living, LLC, BDC, LLC and JAG Publishing, LLC, do not provide tax or legal advice and accept no liability for the information we provide; information is based on our business experience. We are not responsible for information from outside sources and the links we provide to other sources. We provide information to our clients and those who visit our website in search of IRS Negotiating information and general knowledge.
Individuals should cross reference information and forms contained within this resource with the IRS website at: http://www.IRS.gov

Our goal is to provide maximum protection for our clients and readers   through proper information and education based on our experience, while helping them attain their financial goals.

Dedication

This book is dedicated to two people, or should I say one group of people and an individual. First, to the hundreds of thousands of overburdened taxpayers who are notified each year by the IRS that they have back tax issues and see no why out of their situation.

Secondly, to my first mentor – Paul "Gator" Gutierrez, your wisdom and direction in my formative years has made me the man I am today; I will forever be grateful.

Table of Contents

Why I Wrote This Book 12

How to Use This Book for Maximum Success 15

Chapter 1 - Why you should address your IRS obligation as soon as possible? 17

Chapter 2 - First Things 23

Chapter 3 - The Process of Collections 29

Chapter 4 - First Steps 33

Chapter 5 - What to Do if You Owes Taxes to the IRS ... 39

Chapter 6 - Other Forms of Relief 61

Chapter 7 - Levies 69

Chapter 8 - Bank Levies and Attachments 77

Chapter 9 - Abatement of Penalties and Interest & FAQ. 95

Frequently Ask Questions 95

Final Thoughts 109

IRS – Glossary of Terms 114

RESOURCES 139

About The Author

James A. Gage has helped individuals to successfully negotiate with the IRS since 1988 !

James A. Gage has risen to become America's premiere authority on Independent Arbitration and Negotiating with The IRS.

He is the owner of a national debt negotiation firm and has helped thousands of businesses and individuals settle their debts for pennies on the dollar. He has even helped US Congressman and their families settle complex civil and tax litigations!

For over 20 + years, his firm has helped thousands of business owners and individuals SAVE Thousands of dollars off of their debts and taxes.

Early in his investing career he discovered that no matter what you do in life whether investing in real estate, selling a product or service, participating in sales or just the day to day activities of life - you need to know how to Negotiate.

In fact, James was "flipping" real estate in the 1980's, before it was in fashion and the subject of numerous television shows.

Negotiating is truly the" **Million Dollar Skill"** – we negotiate everything from the time we are in the cradle to the grave, so it is vital that everyone master this process, especially when dealing with the IRS.

Having attained financial security, James A. Gage began teaching Independent Arbitration and his "Negotiating System", to students in every major city in the country. To date, thousand have taken his One-On-One training programs and thousands of James's students use his formula everyday to become financially independent and debt free.

James Gage has a diverse background and is uniquely qualified to walk you through the IRS collections process. In addition to actively representing clients before the IRS, James has many professional negotiating designations, along with:

* Masters in Taxation

* Accounting Degree

* Federal & State Arbitrator for over 21 years

* IRS Negotiator with CAF Designation

* Arbitrator for US Congressmen & their families

* Charter Member International Association of Professional Negotiators

* Owns and operates the premiere Independent Arbitration business model that has been adopted by the European Entrepreneurial Association.

Why I Wrote This Book

Many of you might be saying to yourself, why on earth would I be writing a book on how to settle your own IRS debt? After all isn't this the way I make a living by settling individual and business tax delinquencies?
The short answer is Yes!
However, many of these delinquencies can be settled by individuals without the help of a tax professional, and for those that are unable to do so, due to the countless obstacles that may be encountered based on their individual tax situation, I am there to assist in the process and negotiate and settle the obligation in my client's favor. Believe me when I say there is more than enough work out there to keep me and a large army occupied for the next millennium.

My goal with this book is to empower you, the average tax payer, with the knowledge on what the IRS can and can not do, to be confident when dealing with the IRS, and most of all providing education to you, the reader, on what your rights are under United States Tax Law.

Let's face it dealing with the IRS can be very intimidating and the more information you have about their tactics and strategies the better off you will be, and the better settlement you will achieve in the end.

Before we get started you might be wondering why this book isn't hundreds of pages long. After all isn't the United States Tax Code some 6000 pages and 500 million words? Yes, that would be correct, but you don't need any where near 6000 pages to successful negotiate a tax settlement with the IRS; in fact, you will learn this valuable skill in less than 200 pages!

By the way – this is a timeless book! What does that exactly mean? It simple means that it will never go out of date; the way you negotiate with the IRS has not changed in over 90 years. So rest assured, you can read this book with the confidence that the subject matter contained within the confines of these pages is the most up to date information on how to negotiate with the IRS.

So with that said, let's get started….

How to Use This Book for Maximum Success

Lets face it dealing with the IRS can be very intimidating – but it doesn't have to be! If you follow my directions on how to use this book, you will be pleasantly surprised at how simple it will be to approach the IRS. Before we go on, I'm not foolish enough to say that everyone will be successful negotiating with the IRS because each individual's tax situation is different and can have many bends and turns in the road; but what I am saying is that 90 percent of you reading this book should be able to successfully settle your tax obligation – on your terms.

Steps for Success

The first think I would encourage you to do is take advantage of the glossary of terms found in the back of this book; these are the most used terms that the IRS will use when negotiating with you, so it benefits you to get acquainted with them. Next, read this book over several times, take notes on what is applicable to your situation, and refer back to the chapters that apply. Finally, use the resource section in the back of this book, which includes the website in which you may obtain the forms needed to successfully negotiate your tax obligation. In addition, you will find other valuable sources of information that will take your financial life to the next level.

Chapter 1

Why you should address your IRS obligation as soon as possible?

First, you must realize that you are not the only one that has fallen behind on your tax obligations – no matter what the circumstances. In fact, in 2012 the IRS was owed an estimated 3.1 Trillion dollars in back taxes from individuals and businesses! Data from the Internal Revenue Service found that more than 279,000 federal employees and retirees owed $3.4 billion in back income taxes as of tax year ending 2010! The data also revealed that 467 employees of the House of Representatives, or about 4.2 percent of the workforce, owed more than $8.5 million. In the Senate, 217 employees, or about 3 percent of the workforce, owed $2.13 million; and it doesn't stop there. The President's staff was not immune either; people in the executive office of nearly 1,800 workers, about 2 percent owe the government $833,970 in back taxes. So as you can see tax delinquencies transcend every political and economic bracket; status or we you fall on the perceived "food chain" in society is not affected by the taxman's demands on April 15th of each year.

Hopefully now you can plainly see that you are clearly not the only on facing some form of tax delinquencies, in fact, some would say you are in good company when you are fully aware of those who also share your tax problems – doctors, lawyers and even high ranking politicians are not immune.

A few years ago there was a campaign mounted by the federal government to portray the IRS as a user friendly organization waiting to assist tax payers to achieve a win – win situation! Was or is this true? I wish it were, however, the idea that the IRS is out there to cause unnecessary pain, stress and or financial burden on individuals and businesses is equally false to a certain extent.

The fact is that the IRS follows a flow chart made up of statutes, regulations and laws that govern how they apply the tax code to individuals and businesses, which ultimately dictates how they enforce collections.
It should also be noted that the way in which the IRS pursues and enforces individual delinquencies are in most

cases very different from the enforcement of tax law upon businesses.

This book is devoted to the individual tax collection process; if a business tax obligation is what you are dealing with please feel free to visit our website for more information on the services we provide for settlement of those obligations: http://www.NegotiatingWithTheIRS.com .

Three Types of People

There are 3 types of people who have IRS tax obligations – which one are you? Most people fall into one of these categories whether we like to admit it or not. All these people are the way they are because of their environments, whether past or present. Your environment greatly affects who you are as an individual and ultimately has a dramatic affect on all aspects of your life and determines your success or failure. The only one that can judge whether the environment you find yourself is beneficial to you and your goals and objectives in life as an individual is **<u>You</u>**.

I would never take the liberty to paint a picture of you with a broad brush, however, the point of this illustration is to have you, the reader, reflect on their MO (Modus Operandi) or "Method of Operation" and hopefully take that realization of what type of person you are, adjust accordingly and turn a negative into a positive. Remember, small hinges move big doors, so in most cases all that is required of you is small changes, but they must be immediate. Once you come to that realization I would respectfully suggest that you take that information and begin moving in a positive/successful direction on the journey of life – never again experiencing the stress of dealing with the IRS. Now on to the different types of people…

The first type of person is the "Ostrich". Many times this person who assumes the personality of the Ostrich will bury their head in the sand and hope by doing so that everything in life will pass them by, and when they pull their head out of the sand everything will be fine. This in my opinion is the most dangerous of the 3 personalities we will discuss!

The second personality is the "Time Buyer". This person feels if they stall for time as much as possible that the person, person's or organization pursuing them will get tired/frustrated and give up and go away leaving them to go on with their normal daily routine. The truth is that this tactic never works and in most cases causes the individual more pain, either physically, emotionally or financially.

The final personality is where most of the readers of this book fall into, and that is – the "I don't know" personality. These individuals are good people by all accounts and they truly do not know how to handle the situation they find themselves in. Many times due to lack of financial resources they can not obtain the help and direction of a professional, whether an attorney, CPA or accountant that will allow them to make an intelligent decision on how to proceed in solving their tax and or legal problem(s). That is all about to change, at least in relation to your IRS tax obligation; by reading and implementing what you will read in the coming pages of this book.

Chapter 2

First Things

Before we get into the meat and potatoes of how the IRS operates, we must first start with the number one factor that will determine your success or failure when dealing with the IRS! This without a doubt has probably been a very stressful time for you the reader; it's not everyday that you have the IRS sending you threatening letters, telling you they are about to levy your bank account, garnish your wages or attach your home in the form of a lien, or worse force a sale on any real estate that you may own. That being said, you won't be the first and you certainly won't be the last to experience their high pressure tactics, but I'm sure this is of no comfort to you at this juncture.

What I want you to do right now is put everything that has happened to you concerning the IRS and their collection activities on the back burner. In order for you to prevail over the IRS you must have your head in the game, that is, the negotiating game. You must approach the IRS with mental clarity and the proper attitude; approaching the IRS with a chip on your shoulder or in a mental frenzy will be a recipe for disaster.

To illustrate this point I would like to share with you something that happened to me in high school that would forever change my life whenever I have applied it.

The year was 1980, Mr. Lee's 11th grade Science lab at Cooper City High School in South Florida. I was the goofy kid in the third row that loved science, but loved Florida's warm sun more – and we will leave it at that.

Sitting directly in front of me in the second row was a young lady by the name of Joanne Caccitolo. Who, unbeknownst to her, lit up that classroom with her smile and her positive attitude which became infectious to all that surrounded her in that Science class.

I was by no means naïve by any stretch of the imagination, and I knew full well she had the same problems and challenges any 17 year old had in that day and age, but somehow she never showed it or should I say she chose not to show it.

Her positive attitude affected all of us in the classroom and I can say personally, that once again, unbeknownst to her, she helped me turn several unpleasant days into ones that were more bearable – thank you Joanne.

Why on earth am I bringing this up in a tax book? Simple, it is very easy to get depressed about a bad situation, especially when it hits your wallet; this then transfers over into whatever solution you are trying to achieve and your ability to execute it successfully. Believe me if you begin your negotiations from a position of weakness, the negotiations will be fruitless and in many cases you will find yourself in a worst position then when you first started.

In summary, what I am advocating is simple; put that Joanne Caccitolo smile on your face, muster up a positive attitude and absorb the information in the confines of theses pages, and know that with this information you are going to be able to negotiate a settlement with the IRS in your favor.

The second thing you need to do in order to be successful negotiating with the IRS is a Boy Scout saying "be prepared"! There is nothing that spells out disaster dealing with the IRS, besides not having your head in the game, than not being prepared. One of the things I have learned over the years in my tax an arbitration businesses, is that cases are won and lost in the preparation of the case. So with that in mind I want you to stop reading this book and start to assemble a few things that will make your negotiations go more smoothly.

First, write down a brief summary composing of bullet points on how your tax delinquency occurred and the circumstances behind it. Next assemble any letters received from the IRS including notices and demands made upon you, your bank account or real estate owned. If possible have on hand at least the last 3 years of your personal taxes – if filed.

Finally, assembly anything you think might substantiate your request for a payment plan or settlement; such documents could include: death certificate of spouse, bankruptcy filings, state tax delinquencies, foreclosure documents, unemployment verification etc. Keep in mind that this is a starting point and the IRS may request additional documentation, but this will show the IRS that you are an organized individual, and you are serious about settling your tax obligation. Once you have these documents assembled you are now ready to continue reading this book

Now onto your negotiating training, but first we must go over the basic process of the way the IRS does business – that is , the tax collection business…

Chapter 3

The Process of Collections

How Long Can The IRS Pursue Me For Taxes Owed?

This is probably a good way to start this book by going over the statue of limitations for collections on delinquent personal tax obligations. Over the years of negotiating tax debt on behalf of my hundreds of client's I have heard every conceivable explanation by debtors on why they believe that the IRS can not collect on the taxes they owe. This chapter is an attempt to set the record straight and give you the facts so you will be able to assess whether you are considered in a "collectible status" under the IRS statue.

Explanation of the statue of limitations on collections:

The IRS has three years to give you a refund, three years to audit your tax return, and ten years to collect any tax due. Together, these laws are called the statute of limitations. They put time limits on various tax-related actions that you and the IRS can take. We will now discuss each one in detail…

Under the statue you have 3 years to claim a tax refund. This is measured from the original deadline of the tax return, plus three years. For example, your 2005 tax return was due on April 15th, 2006 – 2006 plus 3 is 2009. You have until April 15th, 2009, to file your 2005 tax return and still get a tax refund. If you file your 2005 return after April 15th, 2009, and your refund expires, it goes away forever due to the statute of limitations for claiming a refund.

The IRS has 3 years to audit your tax return or to assess any additional tax liabilities. This is measured from the day you actually filed your tax return. If you filed your taxes before the deadline, the time is measured from the April 15th deadline. For example, you filed your 2006 tax return on February 15th, 2007. The 3- year time period for an audit begins ticking from April 16th, 2007, (the filing deadline) and will stop ticking on April 16th, 2010. On April 17th, 2010, the IRS cannot audit your 2006 tax return unless there is a suspicion of tax fraud. This is why you must file your taxes on time even if you can't pay them! Why? Because it starts the clock ticking on that 3 year window to audit your tax return; so do yourself a favor – file your taxes on or before April 15th of each tax year.

The IRS also has 10 years to collect outstanding tax liabilities. This is measured from the day a tax liability has been finalized. A tax liability can be finalized in a number of ways. It could be a balance due on a tax return, an assessment from an audit, or a proposed assessment that has become final. From that day, the IRS has ten years to collect the full amount, plus any penalties and interest. If the IRS doesn't collect the full amount in the 10- year period, then the remaining balance on the account disappears forever. The statute of limitations on collecting the tax has expired.

Example of the Statute of Limitations

Let me provide an example based on a real life scenario. Mr. Johnson wants to file 6 years of tax returns: 2001 through 2006. All years he has refunds. If he files by April 15th, 2007, Mr. Johnson will receive refunds for his 2003,

2004, 2005, and 2006 tax returns. His refunds for 2001 and 2002, however, have expired.

Let's change the example slightly. Mr. Johnson wants to file 6 years of tax returns: 2001 through 2006. In 2001 and 2002, he could have received a refund. In 2003, 2004, and 2005, he owes. Mr. Johnson cannot apply his 2001 or 2002 refunds as an estimated tax payment towards his 2003 taxes. His refunds have expired. For the 2003 to 2006 tax returns, the IRS has ten years to collect the full tax, plus penalties and interest, from the date Mr. Smith actually files the returns. If Mr. Johnson has a refund for 2006, that refund will be used to pay off his tax debts.

Now that we know about the Statute of Limitations in which the taxpayer and the IRS must follow – let us continue…

Chapter 4

First Steps

Now that we have established that you have a valid tax obligation and you are within the statue of limitations for collection activity, let's go onto the first steps of approaching your obligation.

Ok, you have an IRS tax obligation, so what do you do? Negotiate it of course…

The first step is to gather as much information concerning your tax obligation you have incurred, along with a brief summary on how you fell behind with the IRS (we will use this statement later). Also, you will want to do an inventory on all liquid and projected cash flow which can be used to satisfy the IRS obligation. Don't forget assets such as real estate, equipment and inventory if you own a business as a d/b/a (Doing Business As). This will further facilitate your game plan on what method/strategy you will use to begin paying off the IRS obligation and or enter yourself into a suitable payment arrangement with the IRS.

Next you will want to file out the IRS's Power of Attorney Form 2848 (in the event that you are assisting someone else with their tax obligation) if it is just you or your spouse you can skip sending the form, which is included at our website.

You will fill it out and fax it to the IRS at:

If you live in... THEN use this address... Fax number* Alabama, Arkansas, Connecticut, Delaware, District of Columbia, Florida, Georgia, Illinois, Indiana, Kentucky, Louisiana, Maine, Maryland, Massachusetts, Michigan, Mississippi, New Hampshire, New Jersey, New York, North Carolina, Ohio, Pennsylvania, Rhode Island, South Carolina, Tennessee, Vermont, Virginia, or West Virginia

Internal Revenue Service
P.O. Box 268, Stop 8423
Memphis, TN 38101-0268 * Fax: 901-546-4115

Alaska, Arizona, California, Colorado, Hawaii, Idaho, Iowa, Kansas, Minnesota, Missouri, Montana, Nebraska,

Nevada, New Mexico, North Dakota, Oklahoma, Oregon, South Dakota, Texas, Utah, Washington, Wisconsin, or Wyoming

Internal Revenue Service
1973 N. Rulon White Blvd. MS 6737
Ogden, UT 84404 * Fax: 801-620-4249

All APO and FPO addresses, American Samoa, nonpermanent residents of Guam or the Virgin Islands**, Puerto Rico (or if excluding income under Internal Revenue Code section 933), a foreign country: U.S. citizens and those filing Form 2555, 2555-EZ, or 4563. Internal Revenue Service

International CAF DP: SW-311
11601 Roosevelt Blvd.
Philadelphia, PA 19255 215-516-1017

Note: These numbers may change without notice. **Permanent residents of Guam should use Department of Taxation, Government of Guam, P.O. Box 23607, GMF, GU 96921; permanent residents of the Virgin Islands should use: V.I. Bureau of Internal Revenue, 9601 Estate Thomas Charlotte Amaile, St. Thomas, V.I. 00802.

After faxing and sending a hard copy to the appropriate address, wait 24 hours before you make contact with the IRS – your Power of Attorney needs to get into the system before they will speak with you.

Remember, you only fax in a Power of Attorney if you are negotiate tax delinquencies for someone other than yourself, such as a friend or family member.

At the end of this manual I will go over the step by step process on how to deal with the IRS for maximum success. If you are negotiating for personal liability or that of a spouse you can call the IRS directly at 1-800-829-1040 without filing a form. Now it's time to do battle!

The best way to take this knowledge you will acquire in the coming pages is to pick up the phone and make contact, don't think you can just send a letter of explanation to settle your obligation. Yes, chances are the IRS will request certain documentation be sent to them by fax or U.S. Mail, but the best form of communication with any governmental organization, including the IRS, is the good old phone.

Note: When you send any documentation to the IRS including your yearly tax return, always send it with some form of tracking verification; either by Certified – Signature Required or at the bare minimum "Delivery Confirmation" through the United States Postal Service; this is how I send all documentation to the IRS whether for myself or on behalf of my clients. Why? Because you want to leave a paper trail, it's that simple. This is not only to prove that you have done what was asked of you by the IRS when you are in negotiations, but also is for the purpose of having proof for your own records.

I can not tell you how many of my clients have said they sent a document or tax return in to the IRS, only to have the IRS say they never received it, and if they didn't have proof they sent it, guess what position the IRS will take – it wasn't sent. Also, it is very important that you retain a copy of all tax returns and documentation you send for your records and for the purposes of referring to any items or subject matter the IRS would like to have clarified during the negotiations.

Chapter 5

What to Do if You Owes Taxes to the IRS

This you will find is the longest chapter in the book – and for good reason. There are a number of options open to you as a taxpayer to satisfy your obligation to the IRS! In the coming pages we will go over each of them one by one, from the easiest to the most complex, so grab your favorite beverage and prepare to embark on the first steps to settle your tax obligation – in your favor!

You will hear me say this over and over again in this book, file your taxes when they are due, even if you can't pay taxes owed! Why? It is in your best interest to file your tax returns at your earliest possible convenience.

First, you can claim refunds that can be used to support you and your family. Second, it starts the clock ticking on the 3- year statute for audits and the 10- year statue for collections that we discussed previously. In addition the IRS, in most cases, will not even entertain hearing your proposal for settling your tax obligation until your filings are up to date. So do yourself a favor and file on time; it will make your life a lot easier if you need to deal with the IRS.

One of my long time clients recently asked me if he had to pay his balance due in one payment, or if he could split it up into separate payments? Taxpayers can send in smaller payments using the 1040-V payment voucher that prints out with your tax return.
As long as you pay off the balance before April 15th, the IRS won't charge you any penalties or interest. Even if you cannot afford to pay in full by April 15th, you still have options. You should pick the payment option that will best fit your budget and keep any fees, penalties and interest to a minimum.

Here are your options…

Option 1: Pay by credit card. You will be charged a convenience fee for sending your payment to the IRS, and they will pay interest charged by your bank. Even so, these fees and interest could be lower than what the IRS might charge you on an installment agreement. So do the math first to see which of those two options will be most cost-effective for you.

The benefits of paying taxes by credit card are you can earn rewards when you use a rewards credit card. Take advantage of the rewards that your credit card offers by putting tax payments on your credit card. Watch out, some rewards credit cards have restrictions on the type of purchases and minimum charges before they start rewarding you. You will also have more time to pay your tax bill without filing extra forms. Putting your taxes on your credit card lets you continue to pay your tax bill beyond the April 15 deadline. The IRS has this option, too, but you to file additional forms to take advantage of it.

That being said there are also some drawbacks of paying taxes by credit card in my opinion. First, you will pay interest on the tax you owe. The longer you take to pay your credit card balance, the more you will end up paying in interest. Using a low-interest rate credit card will reduce the amount of monthly finance charges you owe. Secondly, there are convenience fees. When you pay your taxes by credit card, the IRS charges a convenience fee that's 2.49% of your tax bill. If you owe $1,000 the convenience fee will be close to $25. Putting a $10,000 Tax bill on your credit card will cost $250. Obviously, the more you owe in taxes, the higher your convenience fee will be. Thirdly, you can't bankrupt the debt. Income tax is one of the types of debt you can't bankrupt, along with child support and alimony. So, if you are having financial troubles, bankruptcy won't discharge credit card debt incurred from taxes, so it would benefit you to look at some other avenue to get your finances under control.

Finally, your card issuer may think they are a risk. If you must use your credit card to pay your income taxes, the card issuer may see it as a sign that you are having financial trouble. After all, why would you use your credit card if you could afford to pay your taxes? As a result of the increased risk, your card issuer could raise your interest rate, lower your credit limit, or even cancel your credit card.

Assessing the risks

Paying by credit card may give you the flexibility to pay over a period of time, but should be considered just like any other credit card purchase. Remember your balance is still subject to their credit card agreement and interest rate and fees will continue to be dictated by your creditor. Late payments will be included on your credit report, and will impact your credit score, and could affect your ability to get credit cards and loans in the future.

Option 2: Monthly Installment Agreement. This is a formal payment plan you set up with the IRS to pay a fixed amount per month until your taxes are paid off. This is a good option for people who just need some time to pay off their tax. The IRS will assess penalties and interest on any balance that's remains unpaid after April 15th. And the IRS charges a one-time set up fee (from $45 to $105) which is added to your first payment. You can even set up a payment plan right on the IRS Web site using the Online Payment Agreement application.

Setting up a monthly payment plan with the Internal Revenue Service is fairly easy. You can set up an installment agreement quickly either over the phone, by filling out some paperwork, or by using the Online Payment Agreement web application.

A monthly payment plan is generally the easiest way to set up an arrangement to pay off any taxes owed to the Internal Revenue Service. The important thing is to know which installment agreement you qualify for, so that when you talk to the IRS, you'll be able to let the IRS know which type of installment agreement you intend to set up.

That being said, it's important to know that there are four basic types of installment agreements, they are:

1. Guaranteed Installment Agreements

The IRS is required to agree to an installment plan if your balance due is $10,000 or less and you meet all of the following criteria:

- For the previous five years they haven't filed late or paid late.
- All your client's tax returns are filed.

- Their monthly installment payments will pay off your balance in 36 months or less.
- They have had no installment agreement in the previous five years.
- They agree to file on time and pay on time for future tax years.

The minimum monthly payment the IRS will accept is based on a combination of factors which include, but not limited to: how well you can document and substantiate your offer amount and the grand total of your balance due including penalties and interest.

The main benefit of a guaranteed installment agreement is that the IRS will not file a federal tax lien. Tax liens are reported to the credit bureaus and negatively impact your ability to obtain credit. The IRS will also require you to fill out a financial statement (Form 433-F, 433-A, or 433-B) in an effort to analyze your client's current financial situation. If you do not meet the criteria for a guaranteed installment agreement, you should consider a streamlined installment agreement.

2. Streamlined Installment Agreements

The IRS will approve an installment plan for you if their balance due is $25,000 or less, and you agree to pay off the balance in 60 months or less.

If their balance will expire within this five-year period due to the ten-year statute of limitations on collections, then the IRS will require full payment within the remaining statute of limitations. The minimum payment the IRS will accept is the grand total of your balance due (including penalties and interest) divided by fifty.

As with guaranteed agreements, all your tax returns must be filed, and you agree to file your tax returns on time and pay your taxes on time in the future.

The main benefit of a streamlined installment agreement is that a federal tax lien is not required. Furthermore, the IRS will not ask you to fill out a financial statement (Form 433-F) in an effort to analyze your current financial situation.

3. Partial Payment Installment Agreements

If the minimum payments for either the guaranteed or streamlined installment agreements do not fit into your budget, you may be better off considering a partial payment installment agreement for them. This is a type of payment plan where the monthly payment is based on what your client can actually afford after taking into consideration their essential living expenses. Unlike guaranteed or streamlined agreements, a partial payment plan can be set up to cover a longer repayment term, and the IRS may file a federal tax lien to protect its interests in collecting the debts. The IRS will ask your client to fill out a financial statement (Form 433-A, 433 F or both) to report their average income and living expenses for the past three months, plus provide paystubs and bank statements as supporting documentation. Unlike other types of installment agreements, the IRS routinely re-evaluates the terms of partial installment agreements every two years to see if you have the ability to pay more.

4. "Non-Streamlined" Installment Agreements

If your balance due is over $25,000, or your client needs a

repayment term longer than five years, or if they don't meet any of the criteria for a streamlined or guaranteed installment plan.

Such an agreement will be negotiated directly with an IRS agent, and will then be routed to a manager at the IRS for review and approval. This type of agreement is often referred to as a "non-streamlined" agreement as it falls outside the IRS's guidelines for automatic approval of the agreement. The IRS will ask that you provide them with a financial statement (Form 433-A) so they can analyze what's the most you can afford to pay each month towards your client's balance. The IRS will likely ask that you attempt to sell off any assets or take out a bank loan, or get a home equity loan so you can pay off the IRS without needing to get an installment agreement.

The 7 Steps involved in setting up an Installment Agreement

1. Find out how much you owe in unpaid taxes. Call the IRS or get copies of your tax returns to verify the

amount you owe. The amount you owe includes your original tax due, plus penalties and interest.

2. Be aware that the IRS charges user fees to set up a payment plan: $52 for direct debit installment agreements, $105 for new installment agreements without direct debit, or $45 for restructuring or for reinstating a defaulted installment agreement. Low income taxpayers can request a lower fee of $43 (fees are subject to change by the IRS).

3. Fill out Form 9465, Installment Agreement Request. Or use the Online Payment Agreement Application on the IRS Web site to set up a payment plan.

4. Choose a day of the month you are able to make payments. You must make your payment by the same day each and every month. You can choose any day you want between the 1st and 28th of the month.

5. Choose your monthly payment amount. You must pay at least this amount each and every month. You can always pay more, but you should write down the minimum you are willing to pay each month.

6. The IRS will respond to your request in about 30 days.

7. Make payments each and every month. You can pay by check, money order, credit card, EFTPS or automatic withdrawals from your checking account.

Here Are Some Tips:

1. You can request an installment agreement over the phone by simply calling the IRS at 1-800-829-1040. They will set up a payment plan over the phone and send you some paperwork to fill out.

2. The IRS must agree to accept your installment agreement if you meet certain criteria, which requires your total tax does not exceed $10,000 and the monthly payments will pay your tax debt in full within 3 years.

3. The IRS will not approve your installment agreement if you have not yet filed all your tax returns. You will need to file all of their back taxes before requesting a monthly payment plan.

4. If paying by check or money order, they must mail their monthly payment to the IRS about 7 to 10 days

before the due date. This will make sure the IRS receives their payment on time, allowing for any delay in the mail.

What you need to assemble before applying:

- Copies of your tax returns.
- A good idea of how much you can afford to pay each month (making sure that this number is something you can honor each month no matter what happens in your financial life.
- A voided check if you are setting up automatic withdrawal.

Option 3: Defer the payment by requesting non-collectible status. This is usually a good option for people who are facing severe financial hardships and need every dollar they have to provide for their basic necessities. The IRS has been especially helpful this year in dealing with hardship situations, so you shouldn't feel embarrassed about asking the IRS for a forbearance agreement. Penalties and interest will continue to accrue, but the IRS will let you switch to a payment plan once your financial situation improves.

Definition: <u>Currently Not Collectible</u> means that a taxpayer has no ability to pay his or her tax debts. The IRS can declare a taxpayer "currently not collectible," after the IRS receives evidence that a taxpayer has no ability to pay. Such evidence is usually obtained from the taxpayer on IRS Form 433-A, Collection Information Statement. A taxpayer can request "currently not collectible" status by submitting Form 433-A to an IRS Revenue Officer or the IRS Automated Collection System unit.

Once the IRS declares a taxpayer currently not collectible, the IRS must stop all collection activities, including levies and garnishments. The IRS must send an annual statement to the taxpayer stating the amount of tax still owed. This annual statement is not a bill.

While in not collectible status, the 10-year statute of limitations on tax debt collection is still running. If the IRS cannot collect the tax within the 10-year statutory period, then the tax debts will expire.

Option 4: Set up a partial payment plan. If your finances allow you to send some money to the IRS for taxes, but you cannot afford a regular installment agreement, then you might want to consider a partial installment agreement. Like a regular installment agreement, this sets up a plan for sending in a fixed amount per month. The difference is that the monthly payment amount will be based on your ability to pay. The IRS reviews these payment plans every two years, so your payments will likely change over time as your financial situation improves.

Requesting a partial payment installment agreement with the Internal Revenue Service can be easier and less time-consuming than requesting an offer in compromise. In a partial-payment installment agreement, the taxpayer makes regular monthly payments to the IRS, but the payments do not pay off the tax debt in full. After the terms of the installment agreement are fulfilled, the remaining balance of the tax obligation is forgiven in full.

Here's How to Proceed:

1. Find out how much you owe in unpaid taxes. Call the IRS or get out copies of your tax returns to verify the amount that you owe. The amount you owe includes your original tax due, plus penalties and interest.

2. Fill out Form 9465, Installment Agreement Request.

3. Fill out Form 433-A, Collection Information Statement. Form 433-A is used for partial-payment installment agreements and for offers in compromise. Because both programs use the same basic information, this is a good opportunity to find out which tax debt strategy is better for you.

4. Attach three months of backup documentation for all income and expenses reported on Form 433-A.

5. Write a letter stating their request for a partial-payment installment agreement.

6. Submit their written request along with Form 9465 and Form 433-A to the IRS Revenue Officer handling your

case, to the Automated Collection System unit, or to your nearest IRS Service Center.

7. The IRS will respond to your request in about 30 days.

Here Are Some Tips:

1. Congress authorized the partial payment installment agreement option in the American Jobs Creation Act of 2004, so don't let the IRS tell you a partial payment isn't possible.

2. The IRS implemented the partial payment installment agreement option on January 17, 2005. This is a fairly new payment option as far as IRS regulations go.

3. To calculate your monthly payment amount, you will need to know your outstanding tax debt balance, the remaining statute of limitation on collecting that debt, and the reasonable collection potential over the remaining statutory period. You are better offer making an offer to the IRS and let them do the calculations on what they are willing to accept, then trying to read their minds.

4. Once again, before the IRS can approve your partial payment installment, you will need to file all of your tax returns, and be current on your income tax withholding or estimated tax payments. You will need to file any back taxes on their behalf before requesting an installment agreement.

5. A partial payment installment agreement is a contract between you and the IRS. The IRS can re-evaluate the amount of monthly payments every two years.

What You Will Need to Assemble before applying:

1. Copies of your tax returns (only those the IRS requires for consideration for your repayment plan. Never offer more information than the IRS is requesting; this could open another can of worms for you).

2. A good idea of how much they can afford to pay each month.

3. A voided check if you are setting up automatic withdrawals.

Option 5: Request an offer in compromise. This program allows a person to offer a lump-sum payment or a 24-month payment plan to settle their tax bill for less than the full amount owed. The advantage here is that your taxes are paid off for less money. The disadvantage: many people don't qualify for the program, and the IRS scrutinizes every little detail of your finances in an attempt to find out exactly how much you might be able to pay.

What is an Offer in Compromise?

By filing an Offer in Compromise, you are offering to pay less than the full amount of their tax debts to the Internal Revenue Service. The IRS, at its discretion, may accept less than full payment of your tax debts if there is doubt as to whether the IRS could ever collect the full amount of tax debt or if there is doubt as to whether you are actually liable for the tax debt.

How Do You Apply for an Offer in Compromise?

You will need to fill out Form 656, Offer in Compromise, along with Form 433-A, Collection Information Statement.

You will also need to calculate the payment amount you offer to the IRS using the Form 433-A Worksheet.

What are the terms and conditions of the Offer in Compromise Agreement?

The IRS sets forth all the Contractual Terms in an Offer in Compromise.

In a nutshell, you agree to:

1. Pay the offer amount in the Offer in Compromise.

2. File your tax returns on-time and pay your taxes on-time for the next five years.

3. Let the IRS keep any tax refunds, payments, and credits applied to your tax debts prior to submitting your Offer in Compromise.

4. Let the IRS keep any tax refunds that would have been payable to you during the calendar year that your Offer in Compromise is filed and marked approved. If you don't fulfill the terms of the Offer contract, the IRS can, and

probably will revoke the Offer in Compromise and reinstate the full amount of tax liability.

What can I do to protect my Offer in Compromise from being revoked?

If your Offer in Compromise has been approved, you need to make sure the IRS does not revoke your Offer.

At all costs, make sure that you:

1. File your taxes on-time for the next five years.

2. If you cannot file by April 15th, request an automatic extension. Definitely file all taxes by the extension deadline.

3. Pay taxes on-time. If you owe, your taxes must be paid in full by April 15th, therefore make estimated payments or extension payments to make sure you they have a balance due.

If the IRS revokes your Offer in Compromise, they will reinstate the full amount of your tax liability, add on penalties and interest, and begin aggressive collection efforts.

Chapter 6

Other Forms of Relief

In this chapter we will go over alternatives to fulfilling your IRS obligation that may not have been a solution to your situation. That being said, these options should only be used as a last result, and the previous solutions should be used first – if at all possible.

Hardship

If a taxpayer is unable to pay his or her tax liability, and collection activity would create an economic hardship the IRS will consider placing the account in a "hardship" or currently not collectible status. In considering a taxpayer's account for "hardship" status the IRS will compare the taxpayer's monthly gross income against what they call "allowable" expenses. IRS monthly allowable expenses are national averages for food, clothing, miscellaneous expenses, housing, transportation, medical expenses and insurance, as well as proper tax withholding and payments.

These "allowable" amounts vary depending on household size and local standards as well.

"Hardship" is a subjective term and even though a taxpayer's monthly expenses may exceed IRS allowable amounts, it doesn't mean that such status is not warranted or achievable to you. In some cases a taxpayer may have excessive medical expenses in caring for themselves or a loved one, and "hardship status" may still be granted. In all cases, in order to be considered currently not collectible, the taxpayer must provide the IRS with financial information on Form 433A, and supply supporting documentation.

If a taxpayer is over IRS allowable expenses in a situation such as the above example, supporting documentation is even more critical. Understand that the IRS is going to look at your circumstances with a critical eye, and frivolous or fraudulent claims in an attempt to gain "hardship" status carry severe penalties, including criminal charges.

Being placed in "hardship" status is not a permanent solution to a tax problem. A taxpayer that is currently not collectible will have his or her status reviewed every 18 to

24 months by the IRS to determine if "hardship status" is still warranted. However, being considered currently not collectible has strategic planning merit if other viable solutions to a tax problem exist.

For example if a taxpayer is close to the collection statute expiration date on a given tax assessment, being put in "hardship" status for the remainder of that statutory period would result in the relief of those liabilities once that date has passed. Additionally, a taxpayer may be considering bankruptcy and a temporary placement in "hardship" status may allow a taxpayer to wait out any remaining statutory time necessary before those liabilities become dischargeable in a bankruptcy proceeding.

These strategies and techniques require professional analysis in most cases, it's important to consider such advice before making any decisions in handling your tax problem.

How to Receive an Uncollectible Status with the IRS

In order to receive and uncollectible status/hardship from the IRS you must be able to prove that you do not have any assets that would allow you to pay the tax amounts owed;

you must show you only have enough money to pay for your basic living necessities. To do this, you must fill out IRS Form 433-F or 433-A. This is the form used to show all your assets, and is required with most IRS filings because it will give them a sense of your assets that they can liquidate to satisfy your tax liability.

However, the purpose of doing this when filling it out to receive an uncollectible status is to show that you do not have any assets of value that they can liquidate and it would not be worth their time and effort to collect from you.

After the proof is gathered, sending it to the IRS along with IRS Form 433A is the next step. Form 433A is going to require very detailed information about your financial situation, so expect to provide the total monthly costs on all the following:

1. Food

2. Housekeeping Supplies

3. Apparel & Services

4. Personal Care Products & Services

5. Transportation

6. All Utility Costs

7. Rent/Mortgage

So the question must be asked – If I am declared currently not collectible will I ever have to pay the IRS back?

Yes, you will still be required to pay the IRS. When you are declared uncollectible it is only temporary and the IRS will check back with you to see if your financial situation has improved enough for them to collect from you. There are some cases where someone can remain on uncollectible status for so long that the statute of limitations expires on the debt they owe and they legally do not have to pay it anymore.

Bankruptcy

Contrary to popular belief taxes owed to the IRS can be discharged in one type of bankruptcy! That being said, there are 2 types of personal bankruptcy Chapter 7 & 13. With a Chapter 7 Bankruptcy, IRS income taxes can be discharged as opposed to a Chapter 13 where you would have to pay back the debts via a payment plan that lasts 36-60 months. However, in order to wipe tax debts clean you will need to liquidate non-exempt assets, and meet certain qualifications or conditions.

Chapter 7 Bankruptcy Requirements to Discharge IRS Income Taxes

As discussed in the paragraph above, the IRS will not discharge taxes through bankruptcy unless certain conditions are met. These conditions are applicable to tax returns and tax assessments independently.

If any one of the qualifications below are not met, or off by a day or two, the taxes will still be due at the end of the bankruptcy proceedings. Here are the conditions:

➢ **Solely Income Taxes** – Only income taxes can be discharged in bankruptcy as opposed to payroll taxes, and other types of taxes.

- ➢ **Taxes Must Be At Least 3 Years Old** – In other words, the tax debts and their respective returns must be at least three years before filing for bankruptcy. This is often called the 3 year rule which we discussed earlier in this book. Understand that this includes filing extensions as well. So if you received a 6 month extension, then it would be 3 years from the extension date.

- ➢ **Tax Returns Filed 2 Years Before Bankruptcy Filing** – What this basically means is that any IRS taxes you want discharged must have been filed 2 years before you filed for bankruptcy. Therefore, a taxpayer cannot file unfiled tax returns today from 3 years ago and then file for Chapter 7. Substitute tax returns do not count.

- ➢ **Taxes Were Assessed At Least 240 Days Ago** – The IRS needs to have assessed your taxes at least 240 days before you file a petition. Taxes can be assessed more than once in a year. An assessment is when the IRS reviews unpaid taxes, and makes any changes (adding to the balance for example) to the tax return and taxes owed. Therefore, any taxes that don't meet this 240 day rule cannot be discharged.

➢ **No Fraudulent Tax Activities or Evasion** – If you are convicted of tax evasion or fraudulent tax activities, you can kiss qualifying to have your taxes discharged goodbye.

Again, realize in addition to these conditions, you must prove to the bankruptcy court that your last 4 years of tax returns have been filed and you must have a copy of your most recent return. Also, take note that tax liens that have been placed prior to the bankruptcy will not be removed with a Chapter 7 bankruptcy.

Chapter 7

Levies

In this chapter we will discuss what can happen to you if you choose to ignore your tax obligation or are unable to come to acceptable terms with the IRS. Specifically within the confines of this chapter we will discuss levies and what the IRS can and can not levy – and finally what can you do to get them released.

So, what exactly are levies? A levy is a legal seizure of your property to satisfy a tax debt. Levies are different from liens. A lien is a claim used as security for the tax debt, while a levy actually takes the property to satisfy the tax debt.

Assets the IRS Can't or Won't Seize

Not everything you own can or will likely be taken by the IRS levy!   Some items are exempt by law, and others are protected by IRS policy considerations.

Exempt Assets

It should raise your spirits to find out that the IRS cannot use its levy power to seize everything you own (Internal Revenue Code § 6334).

Don't allow yourself to get carried away, as the list of items the IRS can't take is hardly generous, the list covers tax debtors and their dependents (each year's amounts are subject to annual cost of living adjustment):

> ➤ Wearing apparel and school books. This doesn't include luxury wear, like a fur coat, but your cloth coats should be safe as an exemption.
> ➤ Fuel, provisions, furniture, and personal effects up to $7,700.
> ➤ Livestock is included if you are a farmer.
> ➤ Books and tools of a trade, business, or profession up to $3,860
> ➤ 85% of unemployment benefits
> ➤ Undelivered mail; no one knows quite what this means!
> ➤ Railroad Retirement Act and Congressional Medal of Honor benefits. All other pensions and

retirement plans are fair game, with some exceptions for ERISA plans.

➢ Workers' compensation benefits

➢ Court-ordered child support

➢ Minimum exemption amount for wages, salary, and other income.

➢ Certain service-connected disability payments

➢ Most public assistance payments, such as welfare, SSI and VA.

➢ Assistance under federal job training partnerships.

Vehicles are generally not considered personal effects or tools of the trade and are not exempt or partially exempt from levy. However, you can often convince an IRS collector that the vehicle is necessary for your employment and it won't be levied.

Assets the IRS Can Seize as a Last Resort

The IRS can seize anything not listed above; however, IRS policies discourage their collectors from taking certain items. Retirement plans and homes are generally off limits.

As stated above vehicles needed for work or if there is a medical need for transportation on a regular basis are generally not seized, if you can demonstrate there is a necessity for the vehicle. Documentation from an employer or a letter from a physician will go a long way to convince the IRS of your assertion that you need to keep your vehicle.

Retirement Accounts

The IRS can take your Keogh, 401(k), IRA, or SEP. With an employer plan, however, the IRS can only grab it if it is vested—that is, if you have the immediate right to take the benefits. In that case, you will be taxed when it's levied by the IRS but do not have to pay the normal 10% penalty for early withdrawal if you are under age 59H.

In the case of hardship, the IRS can be stopped from taking retirement plans. Contact the Taxpayer Advocate Service immediately and plead that this will create "a significant and undue economic hardship" on you and your family. You may have to enter into a payment plan with the IRS in order to protect your retirement from levy.

Social Security and other federal payments are subject to IRS levy powers. The IRS can seize up to 15% of Social Security payments. If the IRS intends to levy on these payments, you will receive a CP-91 or CP-298 notice.

You and Your Spouse's Income

The tax code allows the IRS to take some—but not all—of your wages or other income. If your income is fairly low or you have several mouths to feed, all of your earnings may be exempt from levy. In most parts of the country, you would be hard pressed to live on the paltry amount the law allows you to keep from the levy.

A portion of each paycheck or independent contractor payment you receive is exempt from IRS levy. The amount you get to keep is determined by the tax code. It is based on the number of exemptions you (and your spouse) can claim on your tax return, plus your standard deduction. (See table in IRS Publication 1494.) The amounts exempt from IRS seizures are subject to annual revisions.

Here is an example:

In tax year 2010, Burt earns $26,000 as a baker for Awesome Bakers. He and his wife, Laurie, owe the IRS $32,000 in back income taxes. If the IRS levies Burt's wages, Laurie, and their two kids are allowed $438 per week exempt from IRS wage levy. All amounts paid to Burt over $438 per week (after income tax and payroll deductions) go to the IRS. If Laurie also worked, the IRS could take all of her net income for their joint tax debt.

Claiming the Wage Exemption

If you claim only yourself—and not a spouse or dependents—you get the one exemption automatically ($172.12 per week). Otherwise, you must file a claim for additional exemptions for others that you support.

To seize part of your wages, the IRS sends a levy notice to your employer or to anyone the IRS suspects is paying you for services as an independent contractor. The recipient of the notice must immediately give you a copy of the notice by law. On the back of the notice is a simple form you must complete to claim the exemption amount to which you are entitled. List your spouse and dependents, date and sign the form, and immediately take it to the IRS office that issued it. After three days, your employer or the business that owed you money as an independent contractor must pay the IRS any nonexempt money owed to you. If the employer or business doesn't, it is liable to the IRS for any money paid you above the exemption

Chapter 8

Bank Levies and Attachments

Real Estate Attachments

As we have learned in previous chapters, if you underpay your taxes, you will receive a Notice and Demand for Payment from the IRS. In most cases, you have 10 days to pay your tax bill in full before receiving a federal tax lien. Once the IRS files a tax lien against you, it will attach to all of your real property. IRS liens automatically apply to property you purchase after the IRS files the lien.

The IRS uses a lien to secure its interest in your property. This makes your tax debt a secured, rather than unsecured, debt. Secured creditors have the advantage of having the legal right to seize your property as collateral due to nonpayment. A lien filed against your home gives you more incentive to pay your tax debt, since the IRS may legally seize your property at any time.

The IRS has a total of three years after you file your tax return to file a federal tax lien against your property. Once the tax lien is in place, it will remain for a total of 10 years. The IRS notes that tax liens release automatically after this 10-year period. Although this is typically the end of the tax lien, the IRS does reserve the right to renew your tax lien for another 10-year period of it sees fit.

Once the tax lien is in place, it encumbers your home's title and will appear in a title search. Since a title search is a standard part of a home sale, you may wish to apply for a lien release prior to selling your home. Although property liens attach to property rather than to the debtor, the IRS allows debtors to request a tax lien release in the event they wish to transfer ownership of their property. It is at the discretion of the IRS whether or not to grant you this release.

If you do not pay your tax debt, the IRS may foreclose on your property at any point during the 10-year period in which the lien is valid. If you stop paying your mortgage, and your primary mortgage lender opts to foreclose on the property, the IRS may "redeem" your home by paying your mortgage lender the amount you owed on your mortgage. It then legally owns the property and any equity you built in the home over time with your mortgage payments.

Primary Residences

As a last resort for dealing with an uncooperative taxpayer, the IRS can take a personal residence, mobile home, boat, or any other place you call home if you owe more than $5,000 (Internal Revenue Code § 6334). For married couples, if only one spouse owes the IRS, the other may be able to stop the seizure.

Seizing your residence requires a court order. If the IRS threatens to do so, contact the Taxpayer Advocate Service immediately. Offer to make arrangements to pay the taxes owed. A second home or vacation place, however, can be levied without a court order.

If all else fails and you are about to lose your pension plan or house, call your Congressperson. A sympathetic staff person, or even the representative, may persuade the

IRS to back off. Again, expect to negotiate a payment arrangement in return for keeping your house.

When your IRS obligation is settled they, the IRS, should send you, usually within 30 days a Certificate of Release. It is important for you to keep track of receipt of this important document for several reasons. If you don't receive this document and verify it has been recorded with the registry of deeds you will not be able to refinance your property, sell your property, obtain a loan, buy a vehicle etc. This will forever cloud your financial history and prevent you from obtaining financial instruments now or in the future. So make sure you address this important document, make multiple copies of it and keep them in a safe place – you'll never know when you will need to produce it.

Here is the process step by step if you have a lien assessed against you personal or a piece of real estate you own:

Getting a Tax Lien Released When Paid in Full

Here is the process in simple terms.

As we have gone over in the previous paragraph(s), the IRS must issue a Certificate of Release of Lien within 30 days after either:

1. The taxes are fully paid, discharged in bankruptcy, or satisfied through an Offer in Compromise, or

2. The lien becomes unenforceable because the statute of limitations for collections has run—usually ten years after the tax was first due (Internal Revenue Code §6325(a)). The lien eventually will become uncollectible after the ten year statute of limitations on collection runs out.

If 30 days pass and no release has yet been issued (not uncommon), then call the IRS Centralized Lien Processing, P.O. Box 145595, Stop 8420G, Cincinnati, Ohio 45250-5595; phone: 800-913-6050. Give the date of your request and your name, Social Security number, employer identification number, address, telephone number with the best time to reach you and tell why the lien should be released, such as the taxes were paid, the lien was filed in error, or the statute of limitations has run.

If requested by the IRS to mail or fax supporting documentation, don't forget to enclose a copy of the tax lien you want released. If you paid the tax, also enclose a copy of an IRS written acknowledgment of payment, an IRS transcript showing payment or a canceled check. For emergencies such as a mortgage loan closing held up by the tax lien, call the Taxpayer Advocate Service. If there is a balance due and you need quick action, be prepared to pay with a certified check, cashier's check, or money order. Alternatively, the IRS should agree to accept payment out of the proceeds of the real estate escrow reflected on the HUD 1 Form.

IRS Bank Levies – Tax Levy or Wage Levy

As I have alluded to throughout this book, the IRS is the most brutal collection agency on the planet. If you desire to deal with them on your own, without the knowledge contained in the coming pages it is akin to going to court without a tax attorney. You will get crushed!! That's where we come in, or should I say you.

An IRS levy is the actual seizure action taken by the IRS to collect back taxes. For example, the IRS can issue a bank levy to take all of your cash in savings and checking accounts in any and all banks that you may do business with! The IRS can levy your wages or accounts receivable and all other sources of income if you own a small business that operates as a d/b/a (Doing Business As). The person, company, or institution that is served the levy must comply. If they do not comply, they too may have daunting IRS legal problems and will need tax relief services. The additional paperwork this person, company or institution is faced with to comply with the levy usually causes the taxpayer's relationship to suffer with the person being levied.

Tax Levies should be avoided at all costs

Levies usually are the result of poor or no communication between the taxpayer and the IRS; this is the case 100% of the time when you have had a levy waged against you! So going forth into the future, remember "the best defense is a good offense" keep the lines of communication open. This will not only serve you well with the IRS, but will also serve you in other areas and venues of your life.

Bank Account Levy

Don't Ignore an IRS Collection Notice, Unless You Want Them to Levy Your Bank Account- Without Your Knowledge!

It should be noted that while the IRS are usually the ones that use this method the most, meaning levies, other creditors have used this method to receive repayment for their debts as well.

For instance, if you have a judgment against you for a credit card debt, the creditor can file for a bank levy to be placed on your account. While state laws differ, in most cases certain monies in your account are exempt including welfare payments, social security payments, VA benefits, child support, etc. If a bank levy has been placed on your account by a creditor, you usually have 30 days to contest the levy (in the case that monies that were seized are exempt). If a bank levy occurs, you should contact the court to find out how to file for an exemption immediately.

When the IRS levies a bank account the levy is only for the particular day the levy is received by the bank - these are generally referred to **"*one shot* "levies**.

The bank is required to remove whatever amount is available in your account that day (up to the amount of the IRS levy) and send it to the IRS in 21 days unless notified otherwise by the IRS. This type of levy does not affect any future deposits made into your bank account unless the IRS issues another Bank Account Levy.

It should be noted that a bank levy can occur frequently and it is not a one time event. A creditor can request a bank levy as many times as he or she would like to until the debt is paid off. Many banks charge a penalty to their customers if their bank account receives a levy. This amount can be over $100 each time. It should be noted that any checks that have been written before the event that have not been cashed will bounce, because your account is frozen. It should also be noted that withdrawals can not occur, but in many cases deposits can.

So if you have received a bank levy and have had your employer deposit money into your account, this money will be seized as well. You will sometime hear this action referred to as an: **Ex parte** which is a Latin legal term meaning "from (by or for) one party to another".

The IRS has special rules and requirements for IRS Bank Levy releases. Not only do they follow the general rules for their wage levies, but they have additional and very specific requirements that must be met before they will release a bank levy. It has been my experience that once all documents and tax returns have been filed, or agreed to be filed, the IRS will usually agree to release the levy.

IRS Wage Garnishment / Levy

An IRS Wage Levy is different from a Bank Levy. This is because wage levies are filed with your employer and remain in effect until the IRS notifies the employer that the wage levy has been released. These are generally referred to as a continuous levy.

The IRS wage garnishment is a very powerful tool and can be financially crippling to you the taxpayer. Once a wage garnishment is filed with an employer, the employer is legally required to collect a large percentage (usually 35-75%) of the taxpayer's NET paycheck and send it to the IRS.

The wage garnishment stays in effect until the IRS is fully paid or until the IRS agrees to release or modify the garnishment. Most wage levies take so much money from the taxpayer's paycheck that the taxpayer doesn't have enough money to live on.

Can you live on $179 a week? That is the amount you will have to live on if the IRS garnishes your paycheck because you owe back taxes. If not, it is in your best interest to negotiate the removal of this form of levy sooner rather than later. **Note: This figure I mentioned above is adjusted up or down based on economic conditions at the time of the Garnishment, and is set by the IRS**.

So what's the best way to handle levies and garnishments? Make contact with the IRS as soon as possible and work out a settlement, but remember it is always better to negotiate when these measures have not been institute by the IRS. Why? Because it weakens your position when negotiating; remember the old saying "possession is 9/10 s of the law". The IRS now has the upper hand so to speak, at least in their mind", to put you into a settlement to recoup their principle, interest and penalties in the shortest time frame possible. If they get any resistance from the tax payer, they will leave the measures they have placed ion the individual in place.

So how do you deal with the IRS in an effort to gain the best settlement plan possible? Approach the IRS with respect and kindness! The worst thing you can do is call the IRS and start venting your frustration; in fact it could make things worse. Calmly explain to them that it was never your intention to run away from your obligation, but due to the circumstances in your life it has been almost impossible to pay your obligation or to initiate a plan to pay – until now.

Once that opening dialogue has been completed it is time to convince them to remove the garnishment/levy against you, this is accomplished by meeting the IRS requirements given to you, such as: making sure all tax filings are up to date (even if you can not make payment for prior year taxes owed), completing any documentation the IRS requires such as Form 433A (personal financial statement), and finally the agreement that you enter into with the IRS representative. During the coarse of your conversation with the IRS, you want to keep repeating that the levy/garnishment is causing a hardship upon you and or your family; try to bring a human element into the mix – remember the IRS as a whole are a bunch of number crunches, and look at numbers all day long rather then associating those numbers and calculations with individuals.

That being said, I'm sure you have some questions concerning levies, so I decided to include the most common questions asked, that will hopefully give you a better understanding of the process.

IRS Tax Levy & IRS Bank Levy FAQ

What is a Levy?

A levy is a legal seizure of your property to satisfy a tax debt. Levies are different from liens. A lien does not have to be filed with the county recorder for the IRS to enforce a levy.

What is a Lien?

A lien is a claim used as security for the tax debt, while a levy actually takes the property to satisfy the tax debt.

What happens if you do not pay your taxes or make arrangements to settle your debt?

The IRS may seize and sell any type of real or personal property that you own or have an interest in. For instance:

The IRS can seize and sell property that you hold (such as your car, boat, or house), or

Levy property that is yours but is held by someone else (such as your wages, retirement accounts, dividends, bank accounts, licenses, rental income, accounts receivables, the cash loan value of your life insurance, or commissions).

When will the IRS usually levy?

Only after these three requirements have been met:

The tax has been assessed and the taxpayer has been sent a Notice and Demand for Payment:

1. You neglected or refused to pay the tax

2. The IRS has sent you a Final Notice of Intent to Levy and Notice of Your Right to A Hearing (levy notice) at least 30 days before the levy.

3. The IRS may give you this notice in person, leave it at your home or your usual place of business, or send it to your last known address by certified or registered mail, return receipt requested.

What is the typical amount levied/garnished from a taxpayer's paycheck?

This is a formula driven process, however, the typically amount is 30-70% of the gross paycheck.

When does an IRS levy of your wages or bank account end?

If the IRS levies your wages, salary, or federal payments, the levy will end when:

- The levy is released
- You pay your tax debt or

- The time expires for legally collecting the tax.

If the IRS levies your bank account, how long must your bank hold funds they have on deposit?

Up to the amount you owe, for 21 days. This period allows you time to solve any problems from the levy. After 21 days, the bank must send the money plus interest, if it applies, to the IRS.

To discuss your case on behalf of your client, call the IRS employee whose name is shown on the Notice of Levy.

If the IRS has placed a levy on your bank account, how long must the bank hold funds they have on deposit?

The bank will hold your funds for 21 day, meaning you have just 21 days to contact the IRS and have them fax over a Release of Levy to your bank. If you don't act quickly to beat the 21 day IRS bank levy deadline, the bank will be required to send your money to the IRS and it will be gone forever.

To discuss your case, you can call the IRS employee whose name is shown on the Notice of Levy.

Chapter 9

Abatement of Penalties and Interest & FAQ

Imagine for a moment that you have satisfied your tax obligation either by lump sum or through an installment agreement. What now? You need to apply for abatement of your penalties, and penalties only! Unfortunately, interest on tax payments may not be abated except in extraordinary circumstances. Interest abatement almost always requires that the taxpayer prove an undue delay by an Internal Revenue Service staff member is the cause, in part, of the interest being assessed – I haven't seen interest being abated in my career of dealing with the IRS. So that is why you always hear the term "penalties can be waived/abated, but interest is statutory".

The IRS will require that penalties and interest be paid in full before any abatement determination is made. Once you pay the bill, the meter stops and you will not have additional interest charges accruing.

An IRS Penalty Abatement request that is sent as a simple letter to the IRS requesting that the IRS Penalties be abated will not be sufficient. The truth is that the IRS receives millions of these simple IRS Penalty Abatement request letters every year and the great majority will be immediately rejected. If an IRS Penalty Abatement request is worth making – **AND, AN IRS PENALTY ABATEMENT IS ALWAYS WORTH MAKING** - an IRS Penalty Abatement is worth making correctly. The IRS receives so many sub-par abatement requests for IRS Tax Relief that a Penalty Abatement that is done with thought and thoroughness stands out in a positive way. The purpose of IRS Penalties is to punish you, the taxpayer, for failing to comply and to send a message to other taxpayers that compliance will be strictly enforced.

Now we will embark on the subject of penalties so you may have a grasp of what type have been assessed upon you and what you can do to recoup penalty payments made.

IRS Civil Penalties

Failure to pay an IRS Tax Liability can result in IRS Penalties and Interest that will compound over years. The interest and the penalties can be as much as 47% per annum. You can count on your IRS back tax debt to **DOUBLE** in approximately three (3) years. This will create an IRS tax liability that will be substantially larger than the initial amount owed. As I said at the beginning of the book, it won't take long for the IRS to bury you in Tax Debt Penalties if you **DO NOTHING**.

IRS TAX PENALTIES as set out in the IRS Code, are imposed to "enhance" voluntary compliance. There are over one hundred-forty separate IRS tax penalty provisions.

Common IRS Civil Law Penalties

1. The accuracy related penalties
2. The IRS penalty for failure to timely file a return
3. The IRS penalty for failure to timely pay a tax, and the frivolous tax return penalties

The fraudulent tax return penalty is set out in IRC Section 6663. This IRS penalty is "75%" of the portion of the underpayment [of tax] which is attributable to fraud. The fraudulent failure to file Tax return penalty is set out in IRC Section 6651(f). This tax penalty also has a maximum 75% rate. The accuracy-related tax penalty is set out in IRC Section 6662. This tax penalty is 20% of the amount of the portion of the understatement of tax attributable to the conduct being penalized.

Accuracy tax penalties include the "negligence or disregard of rules or regulations" penalty, the "substantial understatement of income tax" penalty, the penalty for "substantial valuation misstatement," the penalty for "substantial overstatement of pension liabilities," and the penalty for "substantial valuation misstatement in connection with gift tax or estate tax".

Negligence or Disregard

The term "negligence" includes a failure to make a reasonable attempt to comply with the tax law or to exercise ordinary and reasonable care in preparing a return. Negligence also includes failure to keep adequate books and records. You will not have to pay a negligence penalty if you have a reasonable basis for a position you took. The term "disregard" includes any careless, reckless, or intentional disregard. The penalty is based on the part of the underpayment due to negligence or disregard of rules or regulations, not on the entire underpayment on the return.

The IRS tax penalty for failure to timely file an IRS tax return is set out in IRC Section 6651(a). This IRS tax penalty is equal to 5% of the amount required to be shown on the tax return, per month up to a max of 25% of the amount required to be shown on the tax return.

Substantial Understatement of Income Tax

For an individual, there is a "substantial understatement" if the understatement of tax exceeds the greater of:

- 10% of the correct tax, or
- $5,000

THERE IS INTEREST ON TOP OF THE IRS TAX PENALTIES.

IRS Penalties and Interest will double your original IRS tax liability in approximately 3 years. Not to be redundant, but, this was worth mentioning twice.

Can you afford this? Of course you can't.

The IRS lists numerous situations in which IRS Penalties can be abated with reasonable cause based on your own unique situation.

Reasonable Cause

The IRS considers Reasonable Cause for Penalty Abatement to be:

- Ignorance of the Law (you must demonstrate you made a reasonable effort to learn the law though) Error or Mistake was Made, but you must still show "due diligence, ordinary business care and prudence" had been exercised.
- Forgetfulness, but you must still show "ordinary business care and prudence". Serious Illness, Death, or Unavoidable Absence.
- Unable to Obtain Records
- Incorrect Advice from a competent tax professional

- Incorrect Advice directly from the IRS, written or oral
- Fire, Casualty, Natural Disaster, Other Disturbance

THERE ARE MORE TAX RELIEF "REASONABLE CAUSES"!

With this information, you can Petition the IRS for your IRS Penalty Abatement.

The following information is excerpted directly from the Internal Revenue Manual, IRM 120.1.

1. *Reasonable Cause is based on all the facts and circumstances in each situation and allows the Internal Revenue Service to provide Tax Relief from an IRS Penalty that would otherwise be assessed. Reasonable Cause Tax Relief is generally granted when the taxpayer exercises ordinary business care and prudence in determining their tax obligations but is unable to comply with those tax obligations*

2. *In the interest of equitable treatment of the taxpayer and effective tax administration, the non-assertion*

or abatement of civil penalties based on Reasonable Cause or other Tax Relief provisions provided in this IRM must be made in a consistent manner and should conform with the considerations specified in the Internal Revenue Code (IRC), Regulations (Treas. Regs.), Policy Statements, and Part 120.1.

The IRS Manual goes on to say that ANY REASON will be accepted as Reasonable Cause if it can be shown that the taxpayer exercised ordinary business care and prudence and, despite that, was still not able to comply with their tax obligations.

If you want IRS Tax Relief the IRS needs to know your unique story. How did you find yourself in this situation? Decisions are made by the IRS on an individual, case-by-case basis, which should be very encouraging to you.

Divorce?

Medical Reasons?

Substance Abuse?

Loss of Income?

Death in the Family?

Failed Business?

What Happened to You? Something happened.

In fact, IRS guidelines generously suggest that a Penalty Abatement should be generally granted when the taxpayer exercises ordinary business care and prudence in trying to pay their back taxes.

Reasonable Cause is a subjective matter and the only way to definitively determine whether or not a failure to comply was willful or a result of extenuating circumstances is for the IRS to conduct a thorough investigation of all the facts and circumstances giving rise to the failure. This investigation is triggered by a correctly filed IRS Penalty Abatement Request.

Be aware, if you submit a Penalty Abatement petition and it is denied, you cannot make a request on the same grounds again. An IRS Penalty Abatement request should be done with a Tax Professional at your side.
No matter how well you state your case, the IRS Appeals Officer assigned to your IRS Penalty Abatement request will have some hard questions for you.

The IRS Revenue Officer probably will look at your history of paying your IRS tax. The IRS will ask, "Is this just another attempt to get out of paying?" That is a question that needs to be overcome.

That was certainly a mouth full wasn't it? But believe it or not it isn't complicated at all! In fact all you have to do is file IRS Form 843. Be certain to clear and concise when filling out the form and provide any supporting documentation you might have.

We have found that the IRS abatement process takes 30 – 60 days from when the abatement request is made. If successful the IRS will mail you a check for the penalties you incurred as a result of the delinquent tax obligation. If not successful you can appeal on other grounds; rest assured if the IRS has any questions or need for further documentation they will contact you.

Frequently Ask Questions

Q: Can You Offer to Pay "Pennies on the Dollar" to settle your client's tax debts as advertized on television?

A: The marketing slogan, "pay pennies on the dollar," can be misleading in most cases. In a successful Offer in Compromise, the taxpayer pays less than the full amount taxes, penalties and interest. However, the taxpayer must prove that the amount he or she is paying is equal or more than the reasonable collection potential as determined by the IRS. The reasonable collection potential, broadly speaking, is the IRS' best guess about how much money you could come up with in the next 24 months to pay off your tax debts.

Q: How many Offers in Compromise does the IRS approve each year?

A: The Internal Revenue Service approves a majority of offer in compromise applications each year. In 2008, the IRS approved 89,546 offers, about 86% of the total number of offers received.

The key to a successful Offer in Compromise is making sure that the IRS can process your application, and that you submit complete backup documentation to support your offer.

Q: How long does it take to get an Offer in Compromise?

A: It will take anywhere from 30 days to 1 year to complete the Offer in Compromise process. The flow chart for an Offer in Compromise looks like this:

> ➤ Preparing the Offer in Compromise forms and backup documentation.
> ➤ IRS Processing of your Offer in Compromise
> ➤ Finalizing the Offer and Making Payment Arrangements

Based on the latest statistics, the IRS takes an average of 60- 90 days to process an Offer in Compromise application. Your processing time may be shorter or longer than this depending on how complete of a package of supporting documentation you submit (don't piece mail documentation, unless you think it will take longer than 2 weeks for you to get your documentation together).

Q: Is there a fee for submitting an Offer in Compromise?

A: The IRS charges a user fee of $150 to process an Offer in Compromise at the time of the writing of this book; check IRS.gov to make sure this amount is still in force prior to submitting payment. If you are living below the poverty line, the IRS will waive the $150 fee if you submit Form 656-A to request a fee waiver.

Q: Where do You submit Your Offer in Compromise paperwork?

A: Submit your Offer in Compromise application, forms, and supporting documentation to the appropriate IRS Service Center. See the IRS web site: IRS.Gov, on where to Mail Form 656, Offer in Compromise, or ask the agent you are negotiating with, where they would like you to send said documentation along with a fax number where you can send a fax copy also.

Q: What If You don't Qualify For an Offer in Compromise?

A: If you don't qualify for an Offer in Compromise, you should consider setting up an installment agreement to pay off your tax debts.

Q: Can Penalties and Interest Be Refunded?

A: In many cases after the tax obligation is paid in full you can file for abatement with the IRS to recoup the penalties paid. In regards to Interest that's another story; interest is statutory, meaning it cannot be abated under any circumstances.

Final Thoughts

Hopefully by now you have taken this information and settled your IRS obligations. If that is the case Congratulations on a job well done, if not, good luck on your upcoming negotiations.

Going forward remember to file your taxes on time, even if you owe money! Just because you can't pay your taxes doesn't relieve you from the obligation to file them, and remember it starts the "statutory" clock ticking.

Now I have some good news and some bad news for you! First the good news! Congratulations, you are now equipped with the knowledge to enable you to negotiate your own tax settlement – on your terms.

So you may be asking, what's the bad news? The bad news is that if you live in a state other than: Alaska, Florida, Nevada, South Dakota, Texas, Washington and Wyoming, New Hampshire and Tennessee, you are more than likely going to have some form of delinquent tax issues with your state! Don't panic this is normal! Why?

Because the federal government usually reports back to the state(s) when there has been a tax delinquency that is outstanding and or has been settled. However, it usually doesn't work in reverse, meaning, if your state brings up a tax delinquency they do not report to the federal government (in most cases); doesn't make any sense but as they say "that's the facts and I'm sticking to them".

So that being said, the way that you deal with your state's Department of Revenue is the same way, in many respects, as when dealing with the IRS, but very different in other respects! It has been my professional experience over many years practicing in the tax industry, that when it comes to delinquent taxes owed to the state, their collection activity can be more aggressive and potentially more damaging financially than the IRS – if you can believe that is possible.

I have seen assets seized 24 hours after a notice has been sent to the taxpayer notifying them of their tax obligation! I have seen wage garnishments on taxpayer's employment checks instituted after only 1 demand letter!

They, the state collection department, only gives you 1 or 2 formal notices before they act, and when they do act they usually go for a knock out punch! This could mean immediate garnishment of your wages, freezing bank accounts (AKA placing a lien on your bank account), placing a lien on any real estate property owned, or a combination of any or all of the few venues I have listed. I have seen many of my clients brought to tears as they have shared their experiences of trying to negotiate with their state's revenue department officers and agents. So what's the answer?

My advice to you is simple, before engaging in negotiations stop by my website:

http://www.NegotiatingWithTheIRS.com ,

review our state resource action plan; this will help you navigate your state tax negotiations and cause the process to run smooth. It has been my experience that the state revenue agents can be more difficult to deal with since they perceive themselves as being in competition with the IRS for your available funds to satisfy your tax obligation.

Also don't forget to access our site to download the IRS forms that you will need to settle your IRS tax obligation: http://www.NegotiatingForALiving.com/forms.htm .

To your success,

James A. Gage

IRS – Glossary of Terms

Abatement: A partial or complete cancellation of taxes, penalties or interest owed by a taxpayer. Taxpayers can request that penalties be abated and in many cases, the IRS removes 100% of the penalty. The IRS requires that you have a good reason to request penalty abatement. While IRS procedures for deciding who qualifies for penalty abatement and for what reason seem to differ in each case, the best thing you can do is to request that the IRS abate your penalties by providing the circumstances surrounding your situation.

ACS Automated Collection System (ACS): A computerized collection process for IRS collectors to contact delinquent taxpayers by telephone and mail.

Appeal: A request by a taxpayer who does not agree with an IRS decision. The action of filing an appeal puts the IRS on notice that the taxpayer doesn't agree with the IRS and is seeking a meeting to change the IRS decision. Audits/examination determinations, offers in compromise, installment payment plans, requests for penalty removal, innocent spouse decisions, levies, liens, seizures and just about every type of intrusive action taken by the IRS can be appealed.

Application for Taxpayer Assistance Order (Form 911): Type of appeal used when the taxpayer has exhausted all other means of trying to resolve an issue with the IRS but an agreeable decision can not be reached. This appeal is handled by the IRS's Taxpayer Advocate Service.

Audit: A tax audit is an examination of the tax return you filed with the IRS.

Automated Collection System (ACS): A computerized collection process for IRS collectors to contact delinquent taxpayers by telephone and mail.

Back Taxes: IRS debt from taxes owed from a prior year(s). The IRS assesses back taxes when a taxpayer does not pay taxes when they become due, fails to report all income and taxes on a return, or fails to file a return.

Bank Levy: The IRS can issue a bank levy to take your cash in savings and checking accounts. When the IRS levies a bank account, the levy is only for the particular day the levy is received by the bank. These are generally referred to "one shot" levies. The bank is required to remove whatever amount is available in your account that day (up to the amount of the IRS levy) and send it to the IRS in 21 days unless notified otherwise by the IRS. This type of levy does not affect any future deposits made into your bank account unless the IRS issues another Bank Account Levy.

Bankruptcy: Tax debt may be eligible for discharge in bankruptcy. However, bankruptcy does not always remove all tax liabilities as not all IRS taxes, penalties and interest qualify for complete 100% discharge. In order for a taxpayer to benefit from bankruptcy laws, the taxpayer must determine whether or not tax liabilities must are eligible for discharge.

Certified Tax Resolution Specialist (CTRS): Tax professional who has met the educational, experience, and examination requirements prescribed by the American

Society of Tax Problem Solvers (ASTPS). The CTRS designation is restricted to Enrolled Agents, CPA or Tax Attorney in good standing, who have proven expertise to resolve a wide range of tax problems. The services a CTRS provides to individuals and businesses include securing offers in compromise, installment agreements, penalty abatement, innocent spouse relief, release of liens or levies, non-filer issues and many others.

Collateral Agreement: An agreement sometimes secured by the IRS prior to acceptance of an Offer in Compromise when the IRS wants to cover a future, reasonably possible event, such as a significant increase in income.

Collection Appeal Request (CAP Form 9423): Type of an appeal used when a taxpayer and a Revenue Officer (Collection) do not see eye-to-eye on an intrusive collection tactic that the IRS wants to implement or has already implemented such as a Levy, Lien, seizure or the denial or termination of an installment agreement.

Collection Division: Tax collectors who work out of the IRS Service Center, Automated Collection or District Office.

Collection Information Statement (IRS Forms 433-A, 433-B): IRS financial statements that require disclosure of personal information, particularly assets along with income and expenses.

Correspondence Audit: A correspondence audit is done by mail. The IRS sends you a letter either alleging you forgot some item of income or requests to see the documentation to substantiate a deduction you have taken on your tax return. The most common type is the CP2000 notice, a computer generated notice that you failed to report an item of income. These must be checked closely since the reporting agency, often time the Social Security Administration for W2's, can make typographical errors. If you fail to properly dispute these errors the IRS is free to assess and collect the tax they believe is owed. And if ignored long enough, your only recourse is to pay the tax, penalty, and interest and then sue the IRS in court, an expensive proposition.

Current Market Value: The amount you could reasonably expect to be paid for the asset if you sold it today. You can find out the value from realtors, used car dealers, publications, furniture dealers, or other experts on specific types of assets. You are advised to include a copy of any written estimate with your Collection Information Statement.

Delinquent Tax Return: A tax return not filed by the due date (April 15) or by the dates allowed through the IRS extension periods (August 15 and October 15). Failure to file tax returns may be construed as a criminal (misdemeanor and potentially a felony!) act by the IRS. This type of criminal act is punishable by one year in jail and $10,000 for each year not filed. Regardless of what you have heard, you have the right to file your original tax return, no matter how late it's filed.

Examination: Official IRS term for a tax audit

Expenses Not Generally Allowed: Expenses not allowed such as claiming tuition for private schools, public or private college expenses, charitable contributions, voluntary retirement contributions, payments on unsecured debts such as credit card bills, cable television charges and other similar expenses as necessary living expenses. These expenses can be allowed when you can prove that they are necessary for the health and welfare of you or your family or for the production of income.

Fair Market Value: The price a willing buyer and seller of property would agree on as fair; neither being under any compulsion to buy or sell and both having reasonable knowledge of relevant facts.

Federally Authorized: Only Enrolled Agents, CPA's and Attorneys are allowed to represent taxpayers before the IRS during a formal in house audit. An un-enrolled tax preparer (EA) can defend a client for whom he prepared a tax return during audit but cannot take it to appeals or represent the taxpayer before the collections division. Our members are all federally authorized to represent all taxpayers. We are not affiliated with nor are employees of the IRS. We work exclusively to provide you with the best representation possible in your controversies with the IRS.

Field & Office Audits: Audits are an examination of the tax return you filed with the IRS. The examiner, typically a Revenue Agent, looks for undocumented income and unsubstantiated expenses or deductions. If the audit is performed in the IRS office, it is considered an office audit. These are common for wage earners. If the audit is conducted at the taxpayer's home or place of business, these are field audits. For our clients, field audits are typically conducted in our offices. It is generally too disruptive to have an IRS auditor or examiner hanging around your office for several days.

Freedom of Information Act: A federal law giving citizens the right to see governmental documents, including their IRS files. Freedom of Information documents can be used to explain why, how, when and where a taxpayer's IRS problems started. Having this information is helpful as it discloses the IRS information used to assess taxes, penalties and interest against the taxpayer. Any taxpayer having difficulty in sorting out what the IRS is doing to them should consider using the Freedom of Information Act to obtain their IRS files.

Fraud Loss Recovery: Victims of fraudulent investment schemes, who have lost all or most of their investment, may be eligible to take advantage the United States Tax Code (law) and recoup 30% to 40% of their losses under Internal Revenue Code Section 165 treatment. Most victims of these types of white collar crimes can convert their capital stock losses into ordinary losses and offset them against prior, current and future ordinary taxable income, thereby reducing the taxes paid in those years, and receiving a refund with interest. The process generally involves amending prior year's tax returns and is a highly technical, time consuming and complex process that could prove invaluable to those who've sustained major investment losses due to fraud and white collar crime.

Future Income: The amount the IRS could collect from your future income by subtracting necessary living expenses from your monthly income over a set number of months. For a cash offer, you must offer what you could pay in monthly payments over forty-eight months (or the remainder of the ten-year statutory period for collection, whichever is less). For a short-term deferred offer, you must offer what you could pay in monthly payments over sixty months (or the remainder of the statutory period for collection, whichever is less). For a deferred payment offer, you must offer what you could pay in monthly payments during the remaining time we could legally receive payments.

Garnishments: Garnishment's are ongoing levies. Most common is the wage garnishment in which the IRS takes all but a pittance of your take home pay. The IRS would serve its garnishment on your employer. The employer is required to leave you a preset amount to live on (although you couldn't live on the amount the IRS authorizes) and send the balance to the IRS toward your tax debt.
The garnishment is one of the most effective tools the IRS has to get you to the bargaining table. And most employers hate garnishments since it creates a lot of extra work for their payroll department. Some employers have policies against having unresolved tax debts. We have a strong track record of getting the IRS to release the garnishment.

Innocent Spouse: In order to help taxpayers that are being subjected to IRS problems because of their spouse's (or ex-spouses) actions, the IRS has come up with guidelines for tax relief where a person may qualify as an innocent spouse. This means that if a taxpayer can prove they fit in those guidelines, they may not be subject to the taxes caused by their spouses or ex-spouses. They may qualify for innocent spouse tax relief.

Installment Agreement: The installment agreement is a payment plan between you and the IRS. The IRS has some flexibility regarding the payment amount as long as the debt will be paid off before the statute of limitations expires. If the amount due is small and you are offering large payments, it can be quite simple to get an installment agreement. The agreement comes with some strings attached, such as staying current on the filing and paying of future tax returns for as long as the agreement is in place. Penalties and interest will continue to be charged although the penalty rate is currently reduced during the installment agreement. The IRS charges a nominal fee to setup an installment agreement. For larger debts or those debts involving payroll tax issues the IRS may elect to assign a Revenue Officer (debt collector) to determine the maximum payment they can bet from you.

Jeopardy Assessment: An expedited procedure by which the IRS imposes a tax liability without notifying you first. A jeopardy assessment is rare and used when the IRS believes the taxpayer is about to leave the country or hide assets.

Levies: A levy is the taking of an asset. Most common is the bank levy. The IRS serves a levy notice on your bank for money held in your account. The account is frozen for an amount of money up to the amount owed to the IRS. If there is less in the account than you owe, the whole account is frozen for 21 days. During that time the original amount in the account is locked up. Any new money added is not part of the original levy. At the end of the 21 days the money is transferred to the IRS unless you have obtained a release from the IRS. Most levies are one-shot deals but the IRS can continue to get new levies on a daily basis. They generally don't.; part of resolving tax debts is to obtain from the IRS a release of the levy.

Liens: A lien is merely a statement alleging that you owe a tax debt. It is legally created anytime you owe taxes. It can show up on your credit report, and if the IRS locates property you own, it can be filed against the property. The most common example is a lien filed against your home. Once filed, you cannot sell the asset until the lien is paid off. For houses, the payoff is part of closing documents.

Liquidation Value: The amount the IRS can get from a distress sale of a taxpayer's assets, usually a public auction (typically 70% of fair market value).

Local Standards Maximum allowances for housing and utilities known as "Local Standards" vary by location. Unlike the National Standards, taxpayers are allowed the amount actually spent, or the standard, whichever is less. There are separate allowance amounts for transportation expenses.

National Standards: Allowances for food, clothing and other items, known as the National Standards, apply nationwide except for Alaska and Hawaii, which have their own tables. Taxpayers are allowed the total National Standards amount for their family size and income level, without questioning amounts actually spent.

Necessary Expenses: The allowable payments you make to support you and your family's health and welfare and/or the production of income. This expense allowance does not apply to business entities. Publication 1854, How to Prepare a Collection Information Statement (Form 433-A), explains the National Standard Expenses and gives the allowable amounts. We derive these amounts from the Bureau of Labor Statistics (BLS) Consumer Expenditure Survey. We also use information from the Bureau of the Census to determine local expenses for housing, utilities, and transportation.

Note: If the IRS determines that the facts and circumstances of your situation indicate that using the scheduled allowance of necessary expenses is inadequate, we will allow you an adequate means for providing basic living expenses. However, you must provide documentation that supports a determination that using national and local expense standards leaves you an inadequate means of providing for basic living expenses.

Notice of Deficiency: An IRS notice informing a taxpayer that he or she owes the IRS the amount listed, which is the excess of the taxpayer's correct tax liability for the taxable year over the amount of taxes already paid for such year.

Offer in Compromise (OIC): The "pennies on the dollar" program allows taxpayers to settle their tax debt for something less than full payment. The criteria is fairly rigid and was designed by Congress, not the IRS. It is a pure business decision. The IRS determines what it could liquidate you for and adds to that what it could collect over the next 48 months and arrives at a minimum amount it might accept. The OIC program is a great program for those that qualify. But don't use it lightly since it stops the running of the statute of limitations on collections. Proper preparation of IRS financial statements is the key to a good OIC. And since the IRS is back-logged with Offers, patience is a virtue. But for those that qualify, this is a great program. Offers can be made with a lump sum payment or payments over time (much like an installment agreement). Acceptance by the IRS of an offer does come with strings attached, such as staying current with filing and paying for five years after the offer is accepted.

Offshore Tax Evasion Defense: If you have undeclared funds in foreign bank accounts, now is the time to act in order to reduce your chances of criminal prosecution, minimize severe IRS penalties and work out a structured IRS payment plan. If you believe that you owe back taxes on your foreign accounts, you will need expert tax help (specialized tax attorney, tax resolution firm, etc.) disclosing your foreign funds, obtaining FBAR compliance, and mounting your offshore tax evasion defense.

Payroll Tax Problems: If you owe delinquent payroll taxes, it is important to know that the IRS assigns a higher priority to collecting employment taxes than income taxes. Delinquent payroll taxes will not only generate huge IRS penalties and debt, but may also be considered a federal crime. It is important to resolve payroll tax debt problems swiftly to protect the future of your company.

Penalties: The IRS assesses two types of penalties on late filed income tax returns. The first and most expensive is the failure to file. Any tax return filed after the due date, including extensions, is considered late. The penalty is based upon the balance due with the tax return. The second penalty is the failure to pay. This is also based upon the amount due with the tax return and is calculated from the due date of the return, without regard to extensions. Some people erroneously believe that since they have a refund they don't need to worry about filing on time. However, if the return is ever audited and the result is a balance due, the penalties will be based upon the due date of the return, even if the audit occurs 2 years later.

Pending, Offer: An offer pending starting with the date an authorized IRS official signs Form 656 and accepts your waiver of the statutory period of limitation, and remains pending until an authorized IRS official accepts, rejects or acknowledges withdrawal of the offer in writing.

Petition: A form filed with the U.S. Tax Court requesting a hearing to contest a proposed IRS tax assessment.

Power of Attorney (IRS Form 2848): A form appointing a tax representative to deal with the IRS on your behalf.

Protracted Installment Agreement: An installment agreement that extends beyond the period allowed under IRS issued guidelines.

Quick Sale Value: The amount that can be realized from the sale of a taxpayer's assets when financial and other pressures force the taxpayer to sell quickly, typically in ninety days or less. This amount generally is less than current value, but may be equal to or higher, based on local circumstances typically 80% of fair market value.

Realizable Value: The quick sale value amount minus what you owe to a secured creditor. The creditor must have priority over a filed Notice of Federal Tax Lien before we allow a subtraction from the asset's value.

Reasonable Cause: There are a variety of reasons why taxpayers don't file or pay. Divorce, job loss, death of family members, mental or physical diseases, drug and alcohol problems, dog ate the homework, etc. are many of the reasons why taxpayers fail to file or pay. The law allows for the abatement (removal) of penalties for reasonable cause. Obviously, it is very subjective.

Reasonable Collection Potential (RCP): The total realizable value of your assets plus your future income; the total is generally your minimum offer amount.

Reconsideration: Audit reconsiderations are discretionary on the part of the IRS. However, we have been successful in convincing the IRS to reopen an audit where the taxpayers were poorly represented or new information is now available that was not available at the original audit.

Request for a Collection Due Process Hearing (Form 12153): An all purpose appeal that generally is invoked by filing form 12153, when the IRS has already issued a Lien, is about to issue a levy, and you want to request an alternative collection option that is less intrusive such as an Offer in Compromise, Payment Plan, be declared currently not collectible, request Innocent Spouse Relief, or request a withdrawal, discharge or subordination of a lien. There are certain legal and administrative notices and requirements the IRS must send/meet before a taxpayer can file this type of Appeal.

Running Out: The IRS has 10 years to collect on back taxes unless the time period has been extended, either by consent of the taxpayer or by certain actions of the taxpayer. The most common reason for the statute of limitations to collect to have been extended is when the IRS has no ability to collect on the debt. Typically, this is because the taxpayer was out of the country, had made an Offer in Compromise, or was under the bankruptcy court. During the time the IRS could not legally collect the running of the 10-year statute of limitations is stopped (tolled). Knowing what has happened during the 10 years is critical to knowing when the IRS can no longer dun you for the debt. It is not uncommon for a tax debt to be removed because the time to collect has expired. The IRS is allowed to accept payments from you but they can't dun you for any debt that is outside the statute of limitations for collections.

Statute of Limitation: Legal limits imposed on the IRS for assessing and collecting taxes, and on the Justice Department for charging taxpayers with tax crimes. The current statute of limitation for collection is 10 years from the date of assessment. However, the statute can be extended by certain actions of the taxpayer.

Substitute for Return (SFR): The law allows the IRS to take the income reported to it under your social security number and file a tax return for you. If you were single the prior year, they will file you as single. If you were married the prior year, they will file a return for you as married filing separate. They will not take any itemized deductions you might be legible for nor will they deduct for any dependents you might be entitled for. It will be a very basic return designed to produce the highest amount of tax allowed to the IRS. It is rarely in your best interest. And since you didn't file the return yourself, the year remains open (subject to assessment and collection) forever.

Tax Attorney: Attorney's that specializes in providing tax relief to individuals and businesses with tax problems at the state and or federal tax level. A tax attorney can help taxpayers secure offers in compromise, installment agreements, penalty abatement, innocent spouse relief, release of liens or levies, non-filer issues and many other tax settlements.

Tax Debt Relief/ Tax Relief: Assistance for tax-burdened individuals or businesses who seek a reduction in the amount of taxes owed. Tax relief includes settlements obtained by offers in compromise, installment agreements, penalty abatement, innocent spouse relief, release of liens or levies and other tax resolution strategies.

Trust Fund Recovery Penalty: (formerly called 100-Percent Penalty) A penalty incurred by the responsible person(s) of a business for failure to pay Withholding and Federal Insurance Contributions Act Taxes (Social Security taxes)

Uncollectible Status: A temporary designation by the IRS meaning a taxpayer does not have significant assets or available income, at the present time, from which to satisfy an IRS debt in part or in full. This designation takes a case out of collection, until a taxpayer has an ability to pay.

Voluntary Disclosure: Taxpayers can participate in the voluntary disclosure program before the IRS has initiated a civil or criminal examination or before the taxpayer has received notice of such an investigation. The IRS offers leniency for voluntary disclosure and it is good advice for any American with IRS tax problems to take advantage of this policy. Under this policy, taxpayers have avoided prosecution for possible tax evasion and have had taxes, penalties, and interest reduced.

Waiver: Voluntarily surrendering a legal right, such as the right to have the IRS collection period on a delinquent tax debt which is due to expire at the end of the statutory time period. The IRS may require waivers in exchange.

Wage Levy: The IRS can levy your wages or accounts receivable (if you are d/b/a business) and all other sources of income. The person, company, or institution that is served the levy must comply under Federal law. If they do not comply, they too may have trouble with IRS (legal) problems. Wage levies are filed with your employer and remain in effect until the IRS notifies the employer that the wage levy has been released. These are generally referred to as a "continuous levy". Most wage levies take so much money from the taxpayer's paycheck that the taxpayer doesn't have enough money to live on

Wage Garnishment: A wage garnishment is a levy that the IRS has a right to issue to the employer of a taxpayer who owes the IRS money. The IRS must give proper notice to a taxpayer before it can actually issue the wage garnishment. Proper notice constitutes several form letters and culminates with a letter with an accompanying Final Notice of Levy. Once the notice has been sent to the taxpayer, the IRS can issue a wage garnishment after 30 days from the date of the letter. An employer is legally obligated to comply with the terms of the wage garnishment. However, if the taxpayer is no longer employed or, for some other reason, such as the employer does not owe the taxpayer any money, the employer does not have to honor the wage garnishment. If the taxpayer goes back to work for the employer, then the employer is re–obligated to honor the wage garnishment. Through the wage garnishment, the IRS is allowed to take all of a taxpayer's wages up to a certain amount. The IRS gives the employer a chart that informs the employer of how much they need to send to the IRS. Frequently, the amount the IRS can garnish is up to 80% of a taxpayer's wages.

The wage garnishment is ongoing until the taxpayer contacts the IRS and is able to negotiate a release of the garnishment. The IRS will agree to release a wage garnishment in full if the taxpayer agrees to pay the liability in full, agrees to a payment plan, or can show that the garnishment is causing an economic hardship.

RESOURCES

➢ **www.NegotiatingWithTheIRS.com/forms.htm** : Forms mentioned in this book that will aid you in your negotiations with the IRS.

➢ **www.NegotiatingForALiving.com** : Since you have been successful settling your tax debt, you owe it to yourself to explore how you can negotiate for a living.

➢ **www.TheLeveragedInvestor.com** : Learn how to use leverage in every aspect of your financial life.

➢ **www.JGage.com** : Sign up for your free newsletter on leveraged real estate investing techniques and strategies.

www.ingramcontent.com/pod-product-compliance
Lightning Source LLC
Chambersburg PA
CBHW062013200326
41519CB00017B/4793